World of Whales

Killer Whales

by Katie Chanez

Bullfrog Books

Ideas for Parents and Teachers

Bullfrog Books let children practice reading informational text at the earliest reading levels. Repetition, familiar words, and photo labels support early readers.

Before Reading
- Discuss the cover photo. What does it tell them?
- Look at the picture glossary together. Read and discuss the words.

Read the Book
- "Walk" through the book and look at the photos. Let the child ask questions. Point out the photo labels.
- Read the book to the child, or have him or her read independently.

After Reading
- Prompt the child to think more. Ask: Killer whales are strong hunters. Can you name other ocean animals that hunt?

Bullfrog Books are published by Jump!
5357 Penn Avenue South
Minneapolis, MN 55419
www.jumplibrary.com

Copyright © 2024 Jump! International copyright reserved in all countries. No part of this book may be reproduced in any form without written permission from the publisher.

Library of Congress Cataloging-in-Publication Data

Names: Chanez, Katie, author.
Title: Killer whales / by Katie Chanez.
Description: Minneapolis, MN: Jump!, Inc.. [2024]
Series: World of whales | Includes index.
Audience: Ages 5–8
Identifiers: LCCN 2022054070 (print)
LCCN 2022054071 (ebook)
ISBN 9798885245982 (hardcover)
ISBN 9798885245999 (paperback)
ISBN 9798885246002 (ebook)
Subjects: LCSH: Killer whale—Juvenile literature.
Classification: LCC QL737.C432 C476 2024 (print)
LCC QL737.C432 (ebook)
DDC 599.53/6—dc23/eng/20221110
LC record available at https://lccn.loc.gov/2022054070
LC ebook record available at https://lccn.loc.gov/2022054071

Editor: Eliza Leahy
Designer: Emma Almgren-Bersie

Photo Credits: Musat Christian/Dreamstime, cover; Tory Kallman/Shutterstock, 1, 5; Agami Photo Agency/Shutterstock, 3; Wirestock Creators/Shutterstock, 4; Subphoto.com/Shutterstock, 6–7; Mike Price/Shutterstock, 8, 23tl; Monika Wieland Shields/Shutterstock, 9, 23bl; Danita Delimont/Alamy, 10–11, 23tr; zhu difeng/Shutterstock, 12; VW Pics/Getty, 12–13; Hiroya Minakuchi/Minden Pictures/SuperStock, 14–15; Michael Greenfelder/Alamy, 16–17; Nature Picture Library/Alamy, 18; datmore/iStock, 19; Sylvain Cordier/Biosphoto/SuperStock, 20–21, 23br; Christian Musat/Shutterstock, 24.

Printed in the United States of America at Corporate Graphics in North Mankato, Minnesota.

Table of Contents

On the Hunt 4
Parts of a Killer Whale 22
Picture Glossary 23
Index 24
To Learn More 24

On the Hunt

What is that in the ocean?

We also call orcas killer whales.

But they are not whales.

They are dolphins.

An orca is black and white.

It has a gray saddle.

saddle

Orcas live in pods.
They swim and play.

They hunt.
They swim fast!
They chase seals.

leopard seal

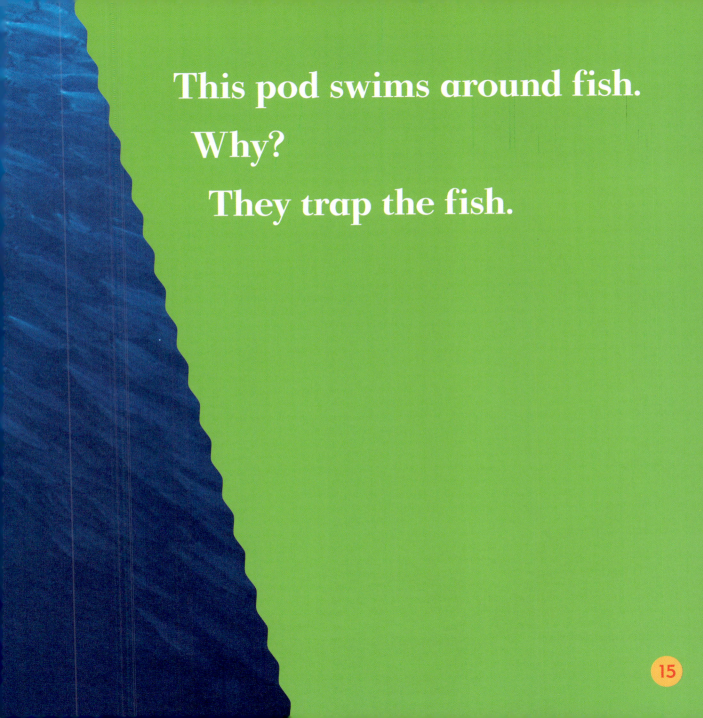

This pod swims around fish.
Why?
They trap the fish.

Then they use their tails.
They hit the fish.

Then they eat the fish!

They use sharp teeth.

tooth

A sea lion is on land. An orca hunts it. The orca swims onto shore. Nice try!

Parts of a Killer Whale

Killer whales can be up to 30 feet (9.1 meters) long. That is almost as long as a school bus! Take a look at the parts of a killer whale.

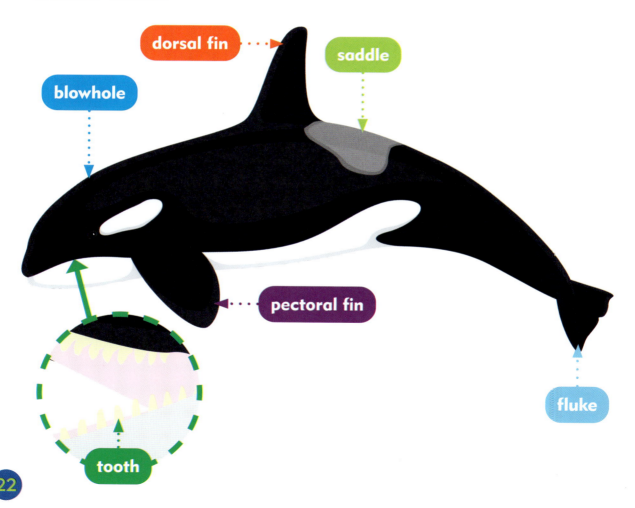

Picture Glossary

dolphins
Ocean mammals that are similar to whales but are smaller.

pods
Groups of whales.

saddle
The gray area behind a killer whale's dorsal fin.

shore
The land along the edge of an ocean.

Index

dolphins 6
fish 15, 16, 18
hunt 12, 21
ocean 4
play 11
pods 11, 15
saddle 9
sea lion 21
seals 12
swim 11, 12, 15, 21
tails 16
teeth 19

To Learn More

Finding more information is as easy as 1, 2, 3.
❶ Go to www.factsurfer.com
❷ Enter "killerwhales" into the search box.
❸ Choose your book to see a list of websites.